T0158368

ARSENIC MON AMOUR

Jean-Lou David and Gabrielle
Izaguirré-Falardeau

ARSENIC
MON
AMOUR

Letters of Love and Rage

Translated by Mary O'Connor

Baraka
Books

Montréal

© Les éditions du Quartz
Publié avec l'autorisation des Éditions du Quartz

Translation © Mary O'Connor

ISBN 978-1-77186-338-4 pbk; 978-1-77186-349-0 epub; 978-1-77186-350-6 pdf

Cover by Maison 1608
Book Design by Folio Infographie
Editing and proofreading: Robin Philpot, Anne Marie Marko

Legal Deposit, 1st quarter 2024
Bibliothèque et Archives nationales du Québec
Library and Archives Canada

Published by Baraka Books of Montreal

Printed and bound in Quebec

TRADE DISTRIBUTION & RETURNS
Canada – UTP Distribution: UTPdistribution.com

United States
Independent Publishers Group: IPGbook.com

We acknowledge the support from the Société de développement des entreprises culturelles (SODEC) and the Government of Quebec tax credit for book publishing administered by SODEC.

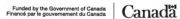

Our environment is barren; it is on the fringes
and the outskirts . . . that life takes hold.

Michel X Côté

To our mothers on the front line.

These letters, peppered with love and rage, are another step in a movement that began long before our time, led by women and men who raised their voices against all odds. To the women who work without pay to demand justice for our community, to the citizens who have spoken out over the years, to those who have paid the price for their commitment, to honest doctors, may this book be used above all as a pretext for giving you a voice again and all the recognition that you deserve.

Dear you,

I hope I won't end up regretting what I'm about to write. Our anger still resonates and rumbles across the town. I watched the stars sparkling over Mount Powell tonight. I tracked the unending sheet of light and the constellations, a narrow maze that imprints in your mind.

As a teenager, I often stood on this rock in the middle of nowhere, this hunchbacked outcrop whose cape appears to challenge the town. There is no beauty in this spot wedged in the bend of an unremarkable industrial park beside Notre-Dame cemetery where the old lie six feet under, lulled by songs about gold. Back then, I failed to notice the path in the stars above. This is where you have the best view of the mine. This is the only point where you can contemplate its entirety with one look, with one movement.

It looks like a tumour that grew there, jammed between the forest and the town. A dirty mammal,

1

a misshapen beast that suffers and moans as it lies on its grey, filthy bedding and exudes layers of waste and black cinders. Its lower body is covered with wounds that ooze murky water as thick as syrup. But when you catch a glimpse of the smelter from above, it suddenly appears beautiful and almost vulnerable.

The way it sparkles at night is truly evil.

*

Every single morning, I see the tall chimneys from the window of my one-bedroom apartment. They're eternal. They're incomparable.

It pains me to admit that nothing here will outlive us. There will be no trace of us. We are a resource legion, a herd headed for certain extinction. We will become the same lowly dust as our ancestors, the same ethereal haze that took them from us. Forgive them for they did not know what wrong we would do.

No part of them will remain. No trace of their gold fever or their Klondike a century ago. Their rush to the district of Nothing. The dust fell on them faster than a puff of chimney smoke that spreads over the town when it's foggy. Our old people are dead, long gone, interred in the muck and the shame of broken dreams.

Now their glorious blindness is a burden that we carry.

Like them, we will not grow old here. The poison that courses through our veins is a seething liquid that cannot nourish the soil. We are from another world.

*

My grandfather came here many years ago, lured by febrile dreams of gold.

One morning, an entire town appeared out of nowhere. Rumour quickly spread across the province and people arrived in canoes and planes and on snowshoes to snatch from the soil what they believed they were owed. They came here to re-enact the grand opening scene of an American western.

That was a gloriously carefree time warmed by *the sun's golden rays*.* Once again, everything seemed possible. It was a never-ending morning at the beginning of time, a dawn that could be unearthed day and night. The sky was fed into the crusher.

A new Babylon appeared in the north. Droves of idle individuals from every corner of the globe, of all

---

* From Richard Desjardins' song *Et j'ai couché dans mon char*.

ethnicities, tribes and religions flocked here to suckle the golden calf's colossal teat.

Grandfather John also tried his luck. He left the already too small fields along the Gatineau River and took an incredible gamble on a genealogical transhumance to the highest summit.

At times, I am astonished by our very existence.

*

Over the past few months, since the spring, I hear a voice that tries to speak through me, a voice I don't yet recognize. Certain mornings, when the chimneys break through the spectacular sky of a rosy dawn, I wonder if it's true that the entire history of humanity is a huge mistake.

I've confessed many times that I believe in God. I look for the obvious signs in the sky of what we should be saying. A yellowish ribbon stretches across the grey clouds. The summer rain that skims my balcony makes my feet wet. I watch those weighed down by life wander in and out of the nearby bar. The tiny house beside the bar on this street used to be a Polish community hall and there was a Ukrainian centre a little farther down.

These people had been scattered by the wind, ousted by wars, famines and epidemics. Displaced persons.

We are also a species displaced by untimely events. This city is not ours.

*

In the pretty neighbourhoods to the west that are lit up by the dying sun and sheltered from the toxic dust, fortunes were also plucked from the ground and patiently piled high.

Abitibi is a wonder that keeps on giving. The gold-bearing Cadillac Fault is the fracture through which the earth gave us life. We are the ungrateful son of a mother who is eternally open and constantly pillaged. Matricide. Destiny has invited us to feast on our own blood.

Abitibi is the last front of colonization in Quebec, the land that God promised to Cain as atonement for his wrongdoing. It's rocky, disjointed and cold, with more flies than a swamp. It's on the periphery of the kingdom, the empire's final breath. Nothing grows there. Prosperity is found through theft and confiscation. Its people are buccaneers who are energized by plundering and shady riverbed deals. This is the last outpost of the French-Canadian spiral, the outer edge of the vortex.

Our madness has never been pushed so far. Our crimes have never resounded as loudly as they do here in this land of vanishing caribou and craters.

*

Last night, I dreamt of old Rouyn, its shacks strewn beside the lake and the echo of gunshots beyond the expanse of calm waters.

Everything here is born of condescension and the conqueror's violence. The shafts stand on the fault's hunched back. We were born in a masculine country.

*

Do you believe in a meteorology of uprising, a science that explains the causal link between sunshine and insubordination? There has never been a rebellion without sunlight. It's a well-known historical fact. The forces of nature are awakened when people's discontent is stoked again in the spring. The sap starts to flow.

I believe that our anger is purely a product of the changing seasons. I saw you once this winter, walking with your head held high in the snowy streets of Noranda, the grey citadel behind you dusted with sparkling snow. I noticed that you didn't lower your gaze. You don't need the sun to renew you, to be proud. You don't hear the warning sounds. You walk and we peek through twitching curtains to watch you pass by. We are envious and malicious, walled in by our toxic silence.

I believe you were born of another sun.

Are you from around here? I'm sorry to ask you that. I'm ignorant, I don't know. I'm not familiar with your family name. My ancestors have never uttered it. You speak like someone whose parents didn't have to sign a pact of silence, but maybe your grandfather bartered his language for a wage and a chance at a life of hardship in another country? Maybe your grandmother wore the shawl of a decent woman, a patient and thrifty spouse?

Forgive me. I don't know anything. *I don't know my neighbour's name. I don't know the names of the stars in the sky or the rivers or the birds.*[*] I only know

---

[*] From Richard Desjardins' song *Y va toujours y avoir.*

what is here. What appears on the unyielding out-crops. I know the taste of the mine's fumes, the three times holy name of the company. I know my mother's anguish and the silence of the men in the family.

I heard that you write books. I also dream of writing. I dream of a book that would be the sum of our thoughts, that would talk of the smoke, the grey spruce trees, the iron monster that snores in the town. A book that would perfectly describe the orange hue of the earth in the tailings ponds, a work that could paint the precise twists and turns of pike in the Kinojévis River, their bellies weighed down by mercury. Most importantly, a book that would also speak of the pink summer sky as the sun slips behind the Kékéko hills in the west.

I hope that you'll write this book one day.

While standing at the door of the meetings this spring, I heard you speak. Your voice was a gently fluttering banner that finally gave me hope. When I saw you, I thought you were like a heroine of yesteryear, the fiery Jeanne la Rouge. I figured you weren't from here, but perhaps you'd come here to stir up our rebellion.

Who are you?

J.-L.
Rouyn-Noranda, July 2022

Dear you,

I might regret what I'm about to write to you. My words are not rooted in tranquility or the reassuring constraints of rationality. They have risen up from ground that was nourished by fervent unrest. Anger, fear, sorrow, tiredness, love and bewilderment all muddled together in a mixture that's both unpleasant and splendid. I'm no longer sure what is beautiful and what is ugly. This smelter that we speak of while being increasingly reluctant to name it—is it beautiful or ugly? It's certainly both simultaneously.

You mentioned Mount Powell. I also went there a few times with a very dear friend, when I was beginning to grasp the incomprehensible love that still binds me to this territory. We didn't look out over the smelter, but on the other side. The side where the sun sets between the sky's frontier and the tree tops, creating a perfect palette of mauve and orange. That's the root of the problem. I've spent a lot of time looking out over this side, the one with magnificent scenery, an endless expanse, silence, and an infinite number of stars. The side that we brag about in advertisements and tourism strategies. When I turned my head, I could see all these narratives as huge stains on the horizon. Ghost towns, displaced neighbourhoods, demolished homes, chimneys spewing promises of premature death in exchange for decent jobs, the cruel and absurd conflict of life versus profit.

With what I've seen, I no longer know how to shrug off the obsession. These days, I am hundreds of kilometres from our region and our town. Where I am writing, there are no towering chimneys, and yet I think of them. They're an ever-present image that I can't erase, surrounded by shadows, smoke, acid, sulphur, copper, arsenic and cadmium. These poison words are stitched together into dangerous mysteries that merge and get caught at the back of the throat in a botched attempt to stifle how far our voices carry.

*

We both know the history behind the quashed rebellion of summer 1934. That was when Ukrainian, Russian, Polish and Scandinavian workers who we called the

"Fros"—the very people who used to meet up on your street—spoke the same language of insurgency and a call for dignity. They'd been chosen because of their reputation as docile and tireless workers, but even the most unwavering obedience cannot survive where the air is unbreathable and daylight is a luxury. Roscoe, the mine manager, could simply ignore their grievances. He just had to prey on the misery of French Canadians and convert them into strike-breakers and add a little tear gas to bring everyone to their knees and make them sing *Long live the company*[*] in unison.

That was not the first time this happened. Once more, money men visited spots where workers wore their fingers to the bone to survive. Their goal was to shift the burden of guilt and divide us, and they succeeded. They believed that the swift repression almost a century ago had, once and for all, destroyed the drive to protest and the absurd desire for freedom that these men had sparked, but I don't agree. It crystallized and permanently sealed the foundations of our resistance. Quiet periods are simply land that is left fallow until the next uprising.

---

[*] From Richard Desjardins' song *Les Fros*.

More and more people are speaking up since the spring and we mustn't forget that this isn't the first time. Voices have been raised for many years and somehow held back in levees of denial. Nothing has changed, but the dams eventually gave way and the worries that constantly intensified finally had the space to spread out and be heard.

When I take the legitimate complaint of these women and men up an octave, it's to elevate the power and fierce beauty of their insurrection. But they're the ones who wrote every word of the indignant lyrics that we sing in a perpetual canon. Many people have said their voices are a cacophony that echoes danger and bitterness. However, I must admit that, among those who speak up, I've witnessed nothing other than love of a land and its children. You can't put a price on abstract things like courage and strength of conviction, but I believe they're the most precious resource on this land. Even what lays at the bottom of this fault that pierces us cannot compare to the solidarity and love of these citizens.

I dream of the day that this will be the story that makes the headlines.

*

You asked me where I come from. It almost pains me to admit that I was not born here and neither were my mother or father. One winter, when I was four years old, we ran aground in a house on the outskirts of the town. We'd come from Montreal via Quebec City, urban centres that I barely remember. At three and a half years old, even before this final move, I learned the lyrics of *Et j'ai couché dans mon char** even though I didn't understand them. I presented an interpretation with questionable pronunciation to anyone willing to listen. I'd like to believe that the day on which *we drove for four hundred miles under a possibly angry sky* was to bring me to where I really came from. I've never been anything other than from Rouyn-Noranda.

> And yet,
> over the past few days, weeks and months,
> I no longer really know
> what that
> means.

---

* Title of a popular song by Richard Desjardins followed by an excerpt.

From this doubt emanates the shooting and chronic pain of a gap in my roots and my identity that is slowly widening.

*

I also believe that spring is a time of rebellion. That's indisputable. Maybe the sun shines its light simultaneously over the obvious injustice and our ability to stand together.

But those with power don't wait for bright days to expand their empire. While reading your words earlier this year, I came to realize the unbelievable conditions under which we built our industrial kingdom, the violent cold of a winter without light. That's how we laid the foundations of the relationship. We must deal with a force that transcends seasonal logic.

I'd like to write the book that you mentioned. I'd like it to answer the voices from the South and even those nearby that sometimes order us to "Just leave if you're not happy." However, I really don't know if I can do it. I don't know how to explain what keeps us here. Is it the almost brutal magnetic pull of Lake Osisko, the physical feeling of emptiness in the forests, the fullness of silence at the end of a country road, the poetry of slightly strange spots that we preserve in our minds like precious secrets even though they're of interest to no one, how time slows down, the value of what can only happen in this precise location, the strength of relationships and achievements that emerge from such extreme isolation? How can we explain these miracles to those who have not witnessed them? How can we say all this while speaking the truth, while recalling the acrid taste that lingers in the lanes of Noranda, the strange colour of the smoke and the yearly land decontamination?

I don't know if I've truly loved this land, or if I simply love the idea I had of it. I know almost nothing about you, apart from your disarmingly lucid words and your fascination—which I can't help but understand—with ghost towns. Indeed, it seems that you have understood, for longer and possibly better than I have, the complex way in which certain things in this Abitibi that we share are intertwined: ugliness and beauty, choice and obligation, nature and its plunder, goodwill and the inevitable, life and death. I used to love and I still love these chimneys. They are reassuring symbols, if you don't measure the magnitude of the real-life consequences and don't grasp how these chimneys and every mine around us embody our beginning and our end. All this time, I've been oblivious to the men and women around me who have handed down from one generation to the next the exhaustion of everyday life in the service of precious metals. I'm afraid of failing to love this place now that I can see the full picture and its contradictions torment me. I'm afraid of trying too hard and misjudging. Since you know the stories behind our current disenchantment, the towering churches that dot our streets, and the names of the men and women who saw this lost North as a promise of a bright future, are you also afraid at times? I try to cling to something resembling certainty. To be itself, Abitibi must exist with its mines. Does this mean it must also (above all?) exist with the people who oppose them?

*

I haven't told you much about who I am, but I think all you need to know is that, despite several attempts, I've never managed to stray far from Rouyn-Noranda. I don't know whether I am truly anything other than an outspoken woman who, strangely, has been spared the repeated failure of attempted rebellions. So, with strength and naivety, I continue to believe in the prolific power of our shared anger, the true value of spreading solidarity, the unlikely ties that unite us, and the hope that we nurture through our shared struggle. There are people in our town who understand this like no other and this is undoubtedly what brings me back time and time again. If the relentless contempt and greed of men in suits ends up bringing these people to their knees and causing their exodus, I think I'd have no choice but to follow them.

What keeps you here in Rouyn?

G.

Sherbrooke, August 2022

Hello again, dear you,

I must tell you that I too don't know what keeps me here and I'm not sure that we should talk about all this. I'm afraid of what will rise up from the bottom of the fault if we look too closely. Thanks for writing to me. I'm home alone in my one-bedroom apartment. Old books are my dearest friends. There's nothing I love more than old paper.

I have a book that mentions my grandfather. *Nos grandes figures du Nord-Ouest québécois.*[*] It was published in 1951 and it's both idiotic and astonishing. It reads like a collection of biblical stories extolling the virtues of local martyrs. Its tone is joyful and it's full of ridiculously grand words and phrases that pop and deflate like balloons. My grandfather was the mayor of Noranda, appointed by the mine's bosses, and the town's first French-speaking mayor. He's referred to

---

[*] Freely translated as *Important Leaders of Quebec's North-West.*

with a great deal of respect. A perfect gentleman, a visionary, and so on. It doesn't say that he was a gloomy drunkard with a thirst for melancholy. We never say such things here. We say all sorts of things that aren't true.

John didn't last a year as mayor. He drank the Noranda Hotel bar dry, chugging it down with a stupendous burst of laughter. He was shown the door and he staggered out. So much for work. So much for truth.

The third chimney was built in 1951. John had stopped drinking then. Noranda already presided over a vast empire. Roscoe, the mine manager, smoked enormous cigars that were more troubling and sickening than the chimneys.

That was the golden age of illusion. The empire had not yet encountered doubt. Change came at such a fast pace that they believed the town would become a sprawling metropolis. Fewer and fewer guys died below ground and they thought they'd reached the end of History. They had domesticated the earth. The company poured the promise of a comfortable American life over the town.

Each worker had a wife, a car, a house. They went to sleep every night with full bellies, satisfied that

they'd ascended from underground before night-
fall. Decades of crisis and tension had finally been
replaced by social harmony, by a Pax Noranda.

*

Noranda and Rouyn are called the twin towns, but
they're not identical. You'd think they had two dif-
ferent fathers. Even though they're conjoined, they're
not of the same gender. Rouyn-hyphen-Noranda is an
inconceivable chimera, an insult to our intelligence.

Even though Noranda is masculine, she is lunar.
She is stern and virile and rules by force. She is direct
and frank and her streets make up perfect blocks. Up
until 1950, she was the company's town. The munici-
pal land register shows that she belonged to Noranda
Mines. She laid down the law there. Liquor licences
were banned and a curfew was signalled at ten o'clock
every night. Under cover of darkness, she became
nocturnal, a hazy figure shrouded in secrecy.

Rouyn is feminine and solar. She is accommodat-
ing and insolent. She is bound by neither faith nor
law. Her lovers are prospectors and bootleggers. She
is a stunning woman who flashes her teeth when

she smiles. She listens to no one. She appears in the nightmares of decent men. No one will ever possess her. No one will ever silence her.

Two towns and two chimneys. The one to the west is very thin and impulsive. She scoffs at the sun. She is Rouyn's protector incarnate. The second one is shorter and stocky and wears a kind of belt around her waist that resembles a watchtower platform. This outgrowth creates a silhouette reminiscent of an erect penis and scrotum. The chimney to the east is more sullen and moody. It personifies Noranda.

*

Empires rise and fall in the same way as other organisms. It's a well-known historical fact. Their mythological beginnings become lost in the mists of time. According to imperial ideology, nothing existed before the empire. It was a terra nullius and ancient peoples were wiped from the territory in a single morning. At the dawn of time, the empire asserted its dominance and shone its light. Once it reached maturity, it quickly developed an obsession with the grandeur and formality that is captured in antique busts of men with luxuriant beards and bulging torsos. This period was the longest and most glorious. The sun never truly sets on the empire.

Little by little, the cogs began to seize up. The empire started to fall short, on a moral level first. Decadence. Almost by accident initially, those who played it safe began to turn against the empire. Then corruption spread throughout the organism and gangrene set in.

One day, the empire was felled by barbarity. The most repugnant individuals were crowned kings. From then on, an eccentric power was wielded by the furthermost outskirts towards the centre. Embolisms jolted the heart of the empire. The new masters were not concerned with honour. They knew that the empire was faltering. They thought only of cutting their losses.

The barbaric leaders in their far-off palatial residences worked on electing petty kings and jesters who would completely surrender. These inconsequential potentates did not exist in their own right. They had no original thoughts. Their lives and their breath fuelled the empire. These cringing lobbyists, travelling salesmen and snake oil peddlers were always ready to bow and scrape, grovel and genuflect. They draped themselves in frayed crimson and faded laurels. They obeyed each firstcomer, yet were too proud to follow orders. They were parodies of themselves. They had many masters. They witnessed the greatness and debasement of the empire. They dreamt of the sun while the empire's capital sputtered and descended into mediocrity.

*

You asked me what keeps me here. It's for all the wrong reasons.

I want to witness our collapse. I want to see the bitter failure of my ancestors' endeavours. I'm still not convinced that all of this was an error. I want some clear evidence. I want to see the bottom of the fault, I want to hear the dry echo of the land, a region drained of its sap. I want to see *money burning on the doorsteps of banks,*[*] the chamber of commerce president dishevelled and distraught. I want to see the satisfied certainty of the nouveaux riches descend into distress. I want to witness our death.

---

* From Richard Desjardins' song *Nous aurons*.

I'd like you to live a long life for us and to fight for our cause when there is nothing left of us. I still don't understand where our path is taking us or why we are here. I'm too closely connected. Every street in this town speaks to me of past events, a monstrous crime that my ancestors are guilty of.

When the time comes for decontamination, rehabilitation, renewal and greening, there will certainly be hordes of optimists on every street corner, buses powered by electricity and enthusiasm, twelve to a seat proclaiming progress. We'll wrap up the tailings sites and scrape together the cinders strewn over the town to build a tall and mysterious mountain that we'll cover with grass and trees. Truckloads of lime will be dumped into the lakes to push the metals to the bottom. It'll all be good as new, as if nothing ever happened here.

Books will hold the only memories of us. You must write very grand books, full of fall colours and the ever-changing shimmer of the sky.

*

Last night, I dreamt of the huge toxic clouds that we've seen in archive photos. I unwound their edges and used them to climb down the thin and perfectly smooth chimney to the west. I descended far below the ground to the blackest depths of the mineshafts. In my dream, I could see the dreadful toiling of the land, the rockbursts that entomb men in the belly of the earth, the dynamite blasts that make tunnels roar and walls crumble.

I saw the horrific fire of 1947 in East Malartic when the boss, who wanted to save the mine, flooded the pit while men were still underground. I dreamt of ferocious strikes and of bread broken amid fiery protest and under red banners. I heard the clink of batons striking street lamps to make women and children cry, the alarm sounding in the fortress on the edge of the town telling everyone to take shelter indoors from the vaporized acid.

I saw the ferocious and formidable struggles that unshackled twenty-somethings, turning buds into whorls of mauve and yellow petals. I also watched devastating setbacks, efforts that we believed had been increased fivefold by a race to the end of the world suddenly flattened and crushed.

I have so much more to say.

*

When my father was a small, tanned and timid boy, the towns faced each other, separated by the lake.

Environmentalists hadn't made their way there yet and we had forgotten the names of trees. Lake Osisko was an open-air dump into which we threw used engine oil and the shells of rusty cars. The mine tipped its molten matte into it at night and the large red fire plumes were a forge that hammered and shaped our silence.

A long time has passed since men and women started to speak out. It began with malformed and painful murmurings that we felt rising from deep within. We couldn't describe what was not yet known. We each felt we'd been wounded, but could not say how. The rain was as acidic as tomato juice and both new and old cars grew spots of rust overnight.

*

In a dream, I revisited the greatest trip of my childhood along 6e rue to the foot of the smelter. The faraway adventures to the corner store on Murdoch Avenue with my big brother holding my hand until we got to the next sidewalk. The incomprehensible chimneys and pipes at the end of perfectly straight streets like snakes hissing down on our young heads.

I relived the carefreeness of those first journeys. My brother was learning to pedal without stabilizers in the lane that leads down to Lake Osisko. I was sitting on my skinny, bony butt in the black gravel, admiring everything he could do better than I could. Our boys-only escapades to the end of the peninsula to hear the seagulls screech. I saw the children's games where we hunted dragons holed up in fortresses guarding their piles of gold. I saw the first rays of spring sunshine during my early years when my already wise brother watched over me. I saw our neighbour standing in the lane wearing a dress, and my friend's big sister combing my blonde hair. I remembered the taste of crab apples from the tree in the yard, picking blueberries with my aunt on the cape below Mount Powell close to Lac Marlon, and wars waged with water pistols and balloons filled with a hose.

And always big yellow clouds. Always an alarm. Always the bitter and reassuring taste. And the ever-present chimneys, as permanent as childhood memories.

*

When I was a kid, my father still worked in an open-pit mine, the Selbaie mine in the town of Joutel. Joutel no longer exists.

Long before then, my maternal grandfather also worked there and my mother remembers the village streets filled with the happy squawking of children.

I was a tree planter for eight years. Eight years of backbreaking labour. One day, I planted trees in the streets and fields of Joutel. I planted a forest where people's lives, hopes and futures used to grow.

Nothing is allowed to last in the Northern mining country. We live for the sake of living, with contempt for the next day and what comes after. There is no future for us. There are mines, the potential of deposits, the estimated production timeline, the increasing and decreasing metal content, the rising and falling cost of gold, the unpredictable market fluctuations, the hubbub of the shut down, the rhythm of the blasts, the hope of reopening, and the spectre of an impending closure. Admittedly, there is all of this, but it's not a future. There is no future in Abitibi. It's the land of the eternal present tense, of dividing up water and time. Our history is drifting towards Hudson Bay and oblivion while our future is siphoned off to the south.

*

On the day when this all ends and they pull down the shutters, when the fault will ring hollow as an empty shell lying on the cinders, I want to be buried beside my family in Notre-Dame cemetery.

My grandfather would not be ashamed of me. I have also worked with my hands. I have also dreamt of gold. I will also have built my own world, a vast one made entirely of paper. I will have consulted every last entry in the town's archives. I will have shrouded the mountain in old, yellowed index cards and made it swallow entire filing cabinets. Maybe that's the moment when I'll find the holy grail.

Then I'll close my eyes so I can hear the smelter's last breath clearly and the creaking of the last wagon. I will return to the bottom of the fault.

J.-L.
Rouyn-Noranda, October 2022

Dear you,

Writing to you forces me to reflect and think about this place that I cherish against all odds, and which shapes my very existence. I'm convinced that we should talk about "all this." We must talk so we can make our rage and our pride heard, so we can mourn while there is something left to mourn, so we can tell others what ties us to this place and plant the hopes and despair that we have borne in our minds and the minds of those who will read our words. Most of all, we must write so that we don't forget. So that these stories of resistance and disappointment can become indelible landmarks for the rest of our lives and for the places where they are told.

    While this seems easy, it's not the case. Replying to you is infinitely dizzying, but by doing so, I'm choosing to make a commitment. I'm writing to you so that I won't revert to silence. This is a safety measure for the woman that I will be in twenty years and beyond, a means of preventing myself from going back on my word, a way to visualize my convictions whenever I feel like faltering and giving up. The motivation behind continuing this correspondence is self-serving. I'm drawing a map for an adult, the woman that I want to become.

*

I'm not alone here. I'm surrounded by beings of light who are eager for justice, creation and everything that comes with it. I live in an apartment with large windows at a bend in a street dotted with mature trees and red-brick houses, where children don't question each breath they take. My attachment to our town and my desire to return there are so strong that they sometimes feel terribly abnormal.

The sun still shines through the living room window as it sets, but the large maple tree has lost its leaves. The first snowfall will hit soon and, along with everything else, we will have to tackle hibernation.

We must speak so that we don't fall asleep.

*

I haven't finished explaining where I come from. I must tell you about my father, Dario.

My father hasn't experienced the total darkness and damp air at the bottom of a mine. His childhood was punctuated by coffee seasons and paths carved in the undergrowth with machetes. Papa was born deep in the mountains of a tiny country that some have never heard of. It's a spectacularly beautiful place of eternal sunshine that engorges fruit hanging from trees, some a hundred years old. It's a patchwork of scents, a long stretch of contrasting landscapes, terra-cotta rooftops, multicoloured facades, impromptu visits and doors that are always open. It's a place that's vibrant. You awaken to roosters crowing and the joyful din of streets coming alive, beeping horns that reverberate and dust stirred up along unpaved streets. Children set off for school in their blue and white uniforms, my aunt Flora starts cooking, her husband Carlos climbs into his huge truck and heads for his plantations, my cousins go to work and to university. Everyday life is similar to ours here, but it doesn't interest many people.

It's a place where Westerners plunder the riches and suppress democracy to strengthen the foundations of their prosperity. Companies from here sack the land and rivers and the lives that they sustain in search of the next big deposit that will sparkle in the daylight. The dissident voices of the communities affected—often Indigenous—are reduced to silence for a while or forever, or their consent is bought off like any other commodity. We rarely see or hear anything about this country in movies, books or news reports except when its suffering drains in an endless series of migrant caravans or during the latest political crisis. That is when Honduras exists, mentioned somewhere in the accent of a Radio-Canada news anchor and their correspondent for the time it takes to say "Such a tragedy" before we return to our blind comfort. It's important that we keep up to date as long as we're at a distance. When I travel to my father's country, my foreigner status is a halo and my hands are filled with gifts. I speak Spanish with nebulous conjugation and roll every second r.

I know little about Honduras beyond Tegucigalpa Airport and Papa's little village. Every morning in the village, my aunts start their day by preparing coffee and round tortillas that look like little moons. They sing, give without keeping track, and love without betraying. They embody devotion, resilience and courage, but these words are never spoken. The sun shines into their homes every day and their rebellious spirit never wavers.

I wish I was more Honduran. I'd like to have that close connection with my cousins, that sense of community that I look for everywhere I go, but struggle to build with them. This might in some small way explain my overly strong attachment to the land where I ended up. If I had to give up half of my roots, the other half would have to push its way to the core.

I learned the basic rules of insubordination from my father and his stories. I listened to each word of protest songs and revolutionary anthems that he struck up and accompanied on the guitar while sitting in his favourite living room chair. I often catch myself humming these songs even when he's not there. Somewhere within me, I have transcribed his stories of rebellions that failed, but were revived over and over with renewed enthusiasm. I know all about falling and starting over, the injustice that fuels exploitation and perpetuates silence, the refusal to be forgotten and the effort required to just exist in this world. On several occasions, I've seen my father cry when he felt powerless against indifference towards his loved ones and the distance that kept him from being with them. However, despite my compassion, I never managed to truly understand the nature of the sorrow that spurred him on.

I haven't experienced even the tiniest fraction of the injustice endured by this family that I admire and cherish, and I often wondered what could possibly link my roots in Abitibi and Honduras since one place oppresses the other. I'm not sure what the answer is, but it reveals an obvious truth nonetheless—the laws of companies are the same everywhere and the only difference is the level of violence.

*

There's an image that regularly pops into my mind. You know it too. Where we're from, you can't escape it. It's a cliché in black and white that adorns historical works. It shows a clever man rowing in his canoe. The strap of his satchel is stretched across his chest, his hat is pushed down on his head. He is looking far into the distance. This is Edmund Horne, the original prospector and providential being around whom the

36

legend of the empire you describe was built. He is presented as a hero in love with a woman who promised him her hand on the condition that he make a fortune, a virtuous soul driven by instinct and perseverance who refused to give up the quest for his holy grail, the very one that he ended up finding a century ago and drained of its copper and gold over fifty long years.

Horne didn't remain at the scene of his discovery. He left with his spoils to spend sunny days far from the empire that he made gush forth from the soil. However, beyond this emblematic photo, his spectre still hovers over us. He invites us to dances at his home on the banks of Lake Osisko, lends his name to the festivities and sporting events that enliven us, makes shiny coins rain down on sectors that would otherwise be left to die of thirst, and repairs the damage that he caused. His presence and his resources multiply endlessly while others disappear or become invisible, so much so that we no longer know which parts of us belong to him. This strange fusion has created the most worrying blind spots and we choose to fall silent rather than risking speaking out against ourselves and those who sustain and entertain us for fear of betraying ourselves and orchestrating our own demise, as if we're not already doing this. Do you think we owe Horne and his hegemonic heritage anything? I don't think so.

We must listen to and respect those who wear themselves out below the ground and toil in the reddish glow of molten copper, but we owe nothing to Horne and neither do they. It's quite the opposite.

*

Dario doesn't descend below the ground, but he digs holes to reveal to the world the objects that embody a history others tried to erase. In the summer, he travels to places that few visit. They bear names in languages that we were not taught. Nemaska, Waskaganish, Oujé-Bougoumou, Chisasibi, Wemindji. So many communities and ignored realities.

Shortly after beginning elementary school, I spent several nights in a row crying because my father was away. He spent weeks at a time with the people of those communities digging and unearthing ancestral land that was to be flooded so we can have working microwaves and dishwashers. These lands are now submerged under metres of water held back by huge dams. History museums contain what was deemed fit to display while history is being erased.

That is what we have done and continue to do across the globe—seize control and take ownership of what is available. You're right. These lands that were invaded in search of riches do not belong to us. It's also true that we owe nothing to Edmund Horne and the company that imposes its will on us. However, we must admit that we owe everything to the land.

*

In Abitibi and beyond, there are so many dying villages that you stumble across as you round bends on neglected roads. I have visited many of them, intrigued by their ephemeral golden ages and why some people chose to remain there and are soothed by the peace of lonely streets. Little by little, the life drains from these towns when a company packs up and leaves, or the illusion of abundance is shattered and governments gradually lose interest. Some store owners lock their doors for the last time, a few more people move away than last year, a road needs maintenance, and eventually the town falls into disrepair.

Small cemeteries bear witness to the lives of those eternally united in the soil that they cleared. However, behind the faded facades and crooked signs are tight-knit communities with a vibrant past and future who refuse the violence of oblivion they were sentenced to.

There are so many abandoned places across the region and a remote location isn't always to blame. We have many shortcomings and it seems that when we overcome them, we build a unique kind of cohesion that strengthens the mesh that binds us.

You say that we won't escape the inevitable fate of empires. I don't want to believe that. I want to believe that we're better than the farcical emperors who refuse to take the blame and the mining claim kings and wealth collectors who see themselves as monarchs and, at a distance from behind their capital and double standards, tell us what's best for us. I want to think this and I hope that we'll shout it out loud. I want to believe that we've built something greater, a community that takes its rightful place without needing to prove itself to the world. I want to think that we're capable of big and beautiful things and of sharing both land and knowledge. I want us to be overly hopeful and eager for meaning, capable of welcoming and open to change. I want to believe that making this a reality is worthwhile. I might be wrong, but I won't be able to forgive myself if I don't try.

＊

I'm sure you figured out that I don't have ancestors who anchor my Abitibi story, but there are characters who I support and love. These lifesaving friendships are renewed every summer on the peninsula as we relive the intense laughter and energy of adolescence. These men and women possess priceless knowledge and lucidity and their voices should be heard far and wide. They are tireless dreamers who look to the future, owners of magical lands, artists with perfectly offbeat visions. Our relationships were cultivated in the after-dark bustle of 8e rue or rue Principale. Some are from here and some are not, but they all love this town and love to help it grow from the inside. Some are mothers with unbreakable convictions who attend every meeting and refuse to be silent because, through their words of protest, they promise a healthier future to those who can picture it. Their words build a refuge where we can shelter when we see only dead ends. I know this, because some of them are our mothers.

We must speak for them. It's our turn to cover them when the sky grows dark so they can rest without fearing the next battle they shouldn't even have to fight, and without letting fatigue dampen their spirit. Dying would be tiresome if nobody tried to save us.

I still have so many things to tell you, to clarify, to ask you. As I write to you, I'm in a rush to immortalize my thoughts and emotions, but it seems I've run out of steam. I'll return in December or January when everything is white and numbed by the cold. I'll have had the time to give this further thought. Streets that once rang with joyful songs will have fallen silent and shop window decorations will be no more than faded outlines. Through the slow-moving passers-by burdened by their down coats, merry and reassuring greetings to familiar faces, and the soothing silence of an afternoon snow storm, I'll delude myself for an instant that I'm breathing in clean air.

We'll probably bump into each other somewhere at the foot of the chimneys, in a place filled with books, warmth and friends. We can continue our conversation there and watch over the fire so it can burn throughout the winter.

There may be no future in Abitibi, at least not the one that we hope for. There may be no solution to prevent our demise or the crises we are condemned to face. Maybe you're right. Maybe we should return to the fault sooner or later and lay down beside our ancestors and forgive them at last. However, if this is our destiny, if fate truly wants the hunger for abundance that drives our species to also bring about its ruin, then so be it. But until then, to ensure that beauty can break the deadlock and survive,

we
will not
shut up.

G.
Sherbrooke, November 2022

Jean-Lou David was born in Rouyn-Noranda in 1993. He is an author.

Gabrielle Izaguirré-Falardeau grew up in Rouyn-Noranda. She is a student, artist and militant.

Mary O'Connor is a Montreal translator who holds a degree from Trinity College, Dublin, Ireland.

This book contains snippets of songs by Richard Desjardins, who we salute.

The "Brûlot"* collection is a playground for annoying pariahs who refuse to be silent. In the shadows of the chimneys that burn day and night, they examine the world with their eyes wide open, make us see what's in our blind spots and, in doing so, challenge our comfort and indifference.

The "Brûlot" collection can offend at times as it seeks to raise eyebrows, flow through us and transform us as literature should—by helping people to broaden their horizons.

---

* *Brûlot* can mean blackfly, firebrand, pamphlet, a scathing attack and more. The original French edition of *Arsenic mon amour* appeared in the *Brûlot* collection launched by Les éditions du Quartz based in Rouyn-Noranda in northern Quebec.

NEW TITLES FROM BARAKA BOOKS

CANADA'S LONG FIGHT AGAINST DEMOCRACY
Yves Engler & Owen Schalk

THE SEVEN NATIONS OF CANADA 1660-1860
Solidarity, Vision and Independence in the St. Lawrence Valley
Jean-Pierre Sawaya

THE LEGACY OF LOUIS RIEL
Leader of the Métis People
John Andrew Morrow

THE CALF WITH TWO HEADS
Transatlantic Natural History in the Canadas
Louisa Blair

THE THICKNESS OF ICE
A novel
Gerard Beirne

Printed by Imprimerie Gauvin
Gatineau, Québec